Olabisi Ojekunle

Factors influencing homeownership amongst civil servants in Ibadan metropolis

Anchor Academic
Publishing

Ojekunle, Olabisi: Factors influencing homeownership amongst civil servants in Ibadan metropolis, Hamburg, Anchor Academic Publishing 2016

Buch-ISBN: 978-3-96067-042-1
PDF-eBook-ISBN: 978-3-96067-542-6
Druck/Herstellung: Anchor Academic Publishing, Hamburg, 2016

Bibliografische Information der Deutschen Nationalbibliothek:
Die Deutsche Nationalbibliothek verzeichnet diese Publikation in der Deutschen Nationalbibliografie; detaillierte bibliografische Daten sind im Internet über http://dnb.d-nb.de abrufbar.

Bibliographical Information of the German National Library:
The German National Library lists this publication in the German National Bibliography. Detailed bibliographic data can be found at: http://dnb.d-nb.de

© Anchor Academic Publishing, Imprint der Diplomica Verlag GmbH
Hermannstal 119k, 22119 Hamburg
http://www.diplomica-verlag.de, Hamburg 2016
Printed in Germany

DEDICATION

I humbly dedicate this work to the Almighty God, the creator of the whole universe and the God of all flesh, for his infinite mercies on me thus far for the successful completion of this research.

ACKNOWLEDGEMENT

First and foremost, my profound gratitude goes to the Almighty God, the one who was, who is and who is to come, for the successful completion of this research work.

My sincere appreciation goes to my supervisor in person of Dr. M.O. Oyewole, whom through his arsenal of knowledge, patience, counselling and encouragements successively guided me to the completion of this research work.

I also appreciate my family for their spiritual, moral, and financial support at all times. Mrs. Ojekunle Kehinde, my amiable and lovely mother who whenever I request for a stick always provide me a tree, Mr. Ojekunle Olabisi Abel, my late daddy I appreciate all your good deeds, and my great siblings, cousins, Aladesuru Odunayo and Akande Mariam, and to my Uncle, Professor Abel Adebayo, I deeply appreciate your all good deeds.

I also want to use this God-given opportunity to appreciate the indelible impacts of the Head of Department, Professor Olatoye Ojo, and my amiable Class adviser in person of Mr. I.O Ayorinde, I really appreciate your counselling and advices through the years.

With a huge sense of commendations, am appreciating the impacts of the department of Estate Management A-lists lecturers, starting from Professor Cyril Ajayi, Professor B.T. Aluko, Professor O.A. Ogunba, Professor A. Olaleye, Dr. O. Adegoke, Dr. T.T. Oladokun, Dr. J.B. Oyedele, Dr. (Mrs.) F.M. Araloyin, Dr. (Mrs.) A.O. Agboola, Dr. C.O. Oluwadamilare Mr. A.A. Odebode, Mr. T.O Babatunde, Mr. G.B. Ekemode, Mr. S.O. Oladokun, Mr. T.O Ayodele, Mr. O.D. Ajayi, I really appreciate your positive academic impacts for the period of my undergraduate programme.

I won't forget to appreciate my wonderful friends and colleagues who were sources of motivation during the course of this research and my academic odyssey, Moshood Saheed, Adeleke Kamaldeen, Abiodun Julius, Abiodun Esther, Abiodun Yomi, Lawal Qowiyu, Adewoyin Adebimpe, Afolabi Albert, Abdulahi Hanafi, Ajewole Martins, Oyewo Mary, Oladeji Morenike, Oladoyin Racheal, Lawal Oyinlola, Babatunde Oluwatosin and others at large, it has been wonderful having caring and resourceful individuals like you.

ABSTRACT

This study examined factors influencing homeownership amongst civil servants in Ibadan metropolis, Oyo State, Nigeria. It identified the socio-economic characteristics of civil servants in Ibadan. It also investigates the housing preferences of civil servants in the study area and identified and examined factors affecting homeownership amongst civil servants in the study area. This is with a view to promoting homeownership.

The study employed the use of self-administered questionnaires to obtain relevant data. A total number 113 questionnaires was used and it was arrived at by taking 15% of the staff capacity of each of the sampled ministries in the Oyo State government secretariat , Ibadan, Oyo State, Out of this number, ninety-five (95) valid questionnaires were retrieved and used for the analysis, indicating a response rate of (84.07%). Data were analysed with the use of frequencies, percentages and weighted mean analysis.

The study revealed that the majority of the respondents were from the ministry of youths and sport, those within the years range of 11-15 years in service are were more than others and it also indicate that the frequency of junior civil servants are more than that of the senior staffs, while those with the age range of 31-40 years are more than other age bracket that was used in this research work and it also shows that there are more female civil servants with a frequency of 54 to 41 of male civil servants, while 74.7% of the civil were married, Most of their academic qualifications were ND (National Diploma), the family size with the most frequency was a family size of 3-4.

The study revealed that the housing of preferences of civil servants in the study was ranked the hierarchical order as follows, Duplex, Condominium, Flat house, Detached house, Bungalow, Semi-detached, Terrace house, Tenement house, Row house while the factors influencing homeownership were ranked in the order below, Costs of building materials, Land acquisition, Personal priority, Salary, Marital status, Loan facilities, Land security, Lending rate, Tribe, Parental home ownership, Gender, Age, Education.

This work recommends that in other to improve and increase homeowners amongst civil servants, government should implement a policy that will make cost of building materials affordable (rebate for importers of building materials), ensure that civil servants salaries are upwardly reviewed as at when and paid promptly, should ensure the mortgage institutions in the country are citizens-friendly, efficient and effective, government should also implement a policy that will make land affordable and secured, and provision of housing loans at a relatively low lending rate should be implemented. These will really help increase number of homeowners the study area.

TABLE OF CONTENTS

TABLE OF CONTENTS FOR FREQUENCY TABLES

CHAPTER ONE

GENERAL INTRODUCTION

1.1 Background to the study

Shelter is one of the basic needs of human, hence more than just a place of habitation but a personal abode of dwelling (personal home) is a dream of an average aged African and it is enshrouded in myth about Africans.

Some homes are constructed by the owners with the intent to occupy, many are inherited, and some are purchased as new homes from real estate developer or an existing home from a previous landlord or owner-occupier.

Homeownership is synonymous to owner-occupier, it is driven by the desire to improve the quality of life and as a dream of an average Nigerians, it is premised on the ease-off on rental prices, peaceful habitation with co-tenants, managing pressures from property managers or landlords, conveniences in terms of alteration, right to modify and use, and the self-fulfillment of owning a home.

According to Fetter (2013), Factors influencing homeownerships are many and broad, but the major influencing factors are; Priority of needs, access to fund, Agboola (1987) in his work recognised finance as part of home development problems. Availability of land, affordability of land, security of tenure etc. Other factors have experienced a steady increase in their impact on home ownership. In a tight money market, homeownership is the first area to suffer, since neither the builder nor the consumer can readily obtain finance for home development.

Homeownerships are increasing in age as well as income levels. This is most likely reflecting the steep increases in the real cost of "affordable housing." One factor that has remained the same is the impact of race. ''No matter what the level of progression of minorities in society, economically many remain below the wealth constraint for home ownership'' (Gyourko and Linneman, 1996).

1.2 Statement of the problem

According to Agbakoba (2015), Homeownership is a desire of an average Nigerian, and most people in Nigeria still find home ownership as a major, it is interesting to note that all governments in Nigeria since Independence have always highlighted homeownership for citizens as a major priority.

Agbakoba (2015) said, "There is a shortage of housing for low - income earners and constantly growing housing demands (due to increase in population) that are not met.'' Unfortunately, banks are reluctant to provide mortgage facilities to low - income earners. In order to solve the home /mortgage challenges described above, the Nigerian Mortgage Refinance Company (NMRC) was established to promote home ownership and increase the availability and affordability of mortgage loans to Nigerians.

The problem of land acquisition has also been identified as a major hurdle that an aspiring home owner has to scale. Because of the cumbersome acquisition process, especially in the urban centers following the enactment of the land use act in 1978 that vested all the land within a state in the governor, getting a piece of land for building homes is tortuously problematic.

Affordability of land is also one of the encumbrances affecting aspiring home owners, prices of land especially in cities are astronomically high and this affect the chances of low-income earners of owning a home.

Lack of Secure Access to Land is also an obstacle and land is a crucial element in the home owning process and its accessibility is vital to efficient and sustainable housing delivery. Land accessibility, according to Omirin (2002) entails land tenure security, land affordability, land availability and the ease with which land is acquired.

Ikejiofor (2005) opines that extensive and intensive literature searches reveal consensus among analysts that accessibility to land poses the greatest difficulty to urban housing production in many developing countries. Evidence abound in urbanization studies in developing countries to buttress the fact that where land has been made available, even the poor have been able to provide themselves with some form of housing (Cheema, 1987, Crooke, 1985; Asiama, 1990).

High Cost of Land Registration and Titling and bureaucratic delay is another hindrance for aspiring homeownership, as seen in the foregoing. The World Bank/International Finance Corporation (IFC) (2006), indicated that when it comes to property registration and transfer, Nigeria has the highest cost of 27.1% of the property value when compared to other developed and developing countries of the world. The report indicated that in Nigeria there are 21 procedures to be followed and the entire process of transfer also last up to 274 days.

These views still hold sway in most Nigeria States as it takes between 2-5 years to obtain certificate of occupancy and high cost of land transfer as observed by Obunadike (2003) "unfortunately, the demand for the services rendered by the lands department cannot be said to be inelastic. Hence with the recent introduction of astronomical high fees for services rendered by the lands department in the state.

After reviewing the existing literatures on homeownership, a gap in literature was discovered and this study focus on filling the detected gap, which is the factors influencing homeownership, especially amongst civil servants in the Ibadan metropolis.

1.3 Aim and objectives

The aim of the study is to examine the factors influencing homeownership amongst civil servants in Ibadan metropolis, Oyo state, with a view to promoting the homeownerships.

The specific objectives are to:

1. evaluate the socio-economic characteristics of civil servants in Ibadan metropolis, Oyo State.

2. examine housing preferences of civil servant in the study area and

3. identify and examine factors influencing homeowners in the study area.

1.4 Justification of the study

The proposition of this study states that there are some salient factors influencing homeownership in the study area. This study therefore intends to critically examine these factors amongst civil servants in Ibadan metropolis.

First, Bana (1991) and Emerole (2002) indicated that inadequate capacity of public housing agencies to deliver housing was one of the key challenges of public housing in Nigeria. Several researches has been done on adequacy and factors influencing public housing in

Nigeria, with only little been done on homeownerships and none been done in the Ibadan metropolis as regards factors influencing homeownership.

Hood (2002) in his ''the determinants of Homeownership: An application of the human capital investment theory to the Home ownership decision'' streamlined his work to the influence of human capital investment theory to homeownership.

He considered factors such as Family income, race, gender, educational attainment, parental home ownership, age, marital status and family size as factors influencing of home ownership.

Authors and researchers had written a lot on homeownership in relation to many other factors without considering influencing factors such as the ease of land acquisition, Affordability of land, access to financial facilities by aspiring homeowners and the effect of land tenure insecurity on aspiring homeowner. The aforementioned influencing factors as regards homeownership is the focus of this research work using Ibadan metropolis, Oyo State, Nigeria as a case study.

The results of this study will therefore offer insights on the factors influencing homeownership amongst civil servants in Ibadan metropolis and will contribute hugely to the existing body of knowledge for residents, stakeholders, the government agencies, and various sectors in the state and beyond.

1.5 Scope of study

The factors influencing homeownership has received various attentions from different researchers in different parts of the country and beyond, and it is mainly because owning a home is a dream of an average Nigerian.

This research work which will be carried out in Ibadan metropolis, Oyo State and it will focus on factors affecting homeownership amongst the civil servant in the study area.

1.6 Study area

This research work will be carried out in Ibadan, Oyo state province of the country (Nigeria). Ibadan is the capital of Oyo State, and the third largest metropolitan area, by population, in Nigeria, after Lagos and Kano, with a population of over 3 million, and the largest metropolitan geographical area. At Nigerian independence, Ibadan was the largest and most populous city in the country and the third in Africa after Cairo and Johannesburg. Ibadan is located in south-western Nigeria, 128 km inland northeast of Lagos and 530 km southwest of Abuja, the federal capital, and is a prominent transit point between the coastal region and the areas to the north. Ibadan had been the centre of administration of the old Western Region since the days of the British colonial rule, and parts of the city's ancient protective walls still stand to this day. The principal inhabitants of the city are the Yoruba's.

CHAPTER TWO

LITERATURE REVIEW

2.1 Housing

According businessdictionary.com (2015), Housing is a building or structure that <u>individuals</u> and their <u>family</u> may live in that meet certain federal <u>regulations</u>.

According Wikipedia (2015), Housing generally refers to the <u>social problem</u> of ensuring that members of society have a <u>home</u> in which to live, whether this is a <u>house</u>, or some other kind of <u>dwelling</u>, <u>lodging</u>, or <u>shelter</u>.

According to inmylanguage.org (2015), the different types of housing available are:

- **Apartment (suite, flat)** - Includes 1 bedroom or more, a kitchen, a bathroom and a living room. A "bachelor" apartment or "studio" is 1 room with a kitchen area and a bathroom.

   Apartments may be in a building or a house. Apartment buildings are high-rise (6-30 storey with an elevator) or low-rise (fewer than 6 storey with no elevator). Apartments are owned by a landlord and are rented to tenants.

- **Condominium (condo)** - A type of home ownership where you buy a unit in an apartment building or townhouse complex, but do not own the land. Each owner pays their own mortgage, taxes, utilities and a **monthly fee** towards property maintenance. Sometimes, you can rent condos from the owner.

- **Duplex** - A house that is divided into 2 separate apartments, one on top of another. The owner of a duplex may live in one apartment and rent the other, or rent both apartments to tenants. A "triplex" is a house that is divided into 3 separate apartments.

- **Detached house** - A single house that is owned by 1 or more persons. Owners may rent 1 or more rooms or the whole house.

- **Semi-detached house** - A single house that is joined to another house with a common wall. The houses are beside each other and attached.

- **Townhouse** - A small house that is joined to a row of other small houses. Townhouses can be bought or rented.

- **Room** - A room in an apartment or house that is rented out. If the tenant shares the kitchen, bathroom and living room with other tenants, this type of housing is called "**shared accommodation**." "Room and board" means that meals are included.

2.2 Housing and housing problems

Housing is a crucial basic need of every human being just as food and clothing and it is very fundamental to the welfare, survival and health of man (Aribigbola, 2006). Hence, housing is one of the best indicators of a person's standard of living and his place in the society. The location and type of housing can determine or affect the status of man in the society. Ajobiewe (2015), noted that shelter is central to the existence of man. He submitted further that housing involves access to land, shelter and the necessary amenities to make the shelter functional, convenient, aesthetically pleasing, safe and hygienic. Hence, unsanitary, unhygienic, unsafe and inadequate housing can affect the security, physical health and privacy of man. Invariably, the performance of the housing sector is one of the yardsticks by which the health of a nation is measured (Garriga, 2006).

The World Health Organisation (1961) stated that a good house should have the following items:

1. A good roof to keep out the rain.

2. Good walls and doors to protect against bad weather and to keep out animals.

3. Sunshades all around the house to protect it from direct sunlight in hot weather.

4. Wire nettings at windows and doors to keep out insects like house flies and mosquitoes.

In essence, housing quality can be judged from the physical appearance of the buildings, facilities provided, quality of wall used in the building construction, eminence of the roofing materials, condition of other structural components of the house, and the environmental condition of the house. Hence, the inadequacy of housing in terms of quality and quantity results in poor standard of the environment.

Housing problems abound in Nigeria both in rural areas and urban centres. The problem in the rural areas has to do with qualitative housing while the problem in the urban centre is quantitative in nature. Housing problems in the rural areas are connected with qualitative deficiencies like place, degree of goodness and the value of the house.

Wahab (1993) declared that rural housing is incomplete because social services cannot be adequately linked with them. He submitted further that the social services required with housing include electricity, water supply, as well as transportation facilities. All these are deficient in rural housing. On the other hand, urban housing problems include homelessness slum dwelling, squatting and overcrowding.

High rate of urbanization, ever-increasing population of urban dwellers in conjunction with the increasing social expectations of the people are all responsible for housing problems in Nigeria. Ibimilua and Ibimilua (2011) identified the problems of urbanization as inadequate housing, unplanned development, and improper maintenance of existing structures, aging, and absence of social infrastructure, waste management menace, crime, and health hazard.

Additionally, the houses in the urban core areas are characterized by inadequate infrastructural facilities, poor ventilation, non-availability of in-built toilet and kitchen, as well as poor refuse disposal system. Other problems that are associated with urban housing are lack of effective planning, development of shanty towns, and availability of dilapidated houses.

Generally, housing in Nigeria is bombarded with problems like poverty, discrimination against the use of indigenous materials, ineffective housing finance, inadequate financial instrument for mobilization of funds, high cost of building materials shortage of infrastructural facilities, as well as the bureaucracies in land acquisition, processing of certificate of occupancy (C of O), and approval of building plans.

Other constraints to housing development, maintenance and delivery are lack of effective planning, ineffective government programmes and policies, uncontrolled private sector participation, weak institutional frameworks and poor research and development into housing. In addition to the earlier mentioned problems, Agbola (1998) submitted that housing is inextricably interrelated with broader issues of inflation, income policy, and perplexing range of difficult social and economic trends. All these challenges culminated in the ever-increasing demand that cannot be met by supply.

Researches (Balchin, 1995; Onibokun, 1990; Baer, 1991; Mtafu et al, 2011; Aribigbola, 2006; Kabir, 2004; Charles, 2003) have suggested that housing problems cannot be eradicated. Even the developed countries still have some pockets of homeless people. In Nigeria, the problems of squatting, forced eviction and homelessness are common phenomena in major urban centres like Lagos, Kano, Port Harcourt, Ibadan, Oweri and Kaduna. With a population of over 140 million people and over 35% living in the cities, the housing problem is very cumbersome. In fact, Falade (2007) projected that given an annual population increment of 2.8% and all other factors being equal, more than 62% will be living in urban centres in Nigeria by year 2020. Presently, urban centres are characterized by shortage of housing quantitatively, slum dwelling, squatter settlements, inadequate infrastructural amenities, squalor, overcrowding and generally poor living condition.

At the national level, housing is characterized by abandoned projects, non-implementation of housing policies and neglect of the poor. Mtafu et al, 2011 pointed out that low income level and affordability are the major challenges.

Other problems of housing delivery in Nigeria are connected with the imperfections in policy instruments and its implications. The problems can equally be traced to administrative bottlenecks, in housing delivery.

2.3 Factors determining home ownership

According Hood (2014), the factors in home ownership decision include race, gender and educational attainment, age, marital status and family size. Some factors, such as net family income and parental home ownership, affect both benefits and costs.

1. **Net Family Income:** The net family income has both a direct and indirect influence on the home ownership decision. It is related directly in that as the net income rises within a family, the taste for home ownership also rises. A higher income has more potential to cover the initial costs incurred by home ownership. Income is indirectly related because as income rises, the costs of home ownership decreases. Given that costs are constant, as income increases, the costs become an increasingly smaller proportion of the income. This creates greater value of investment in a non-taxed asset for investors in higher income brackets (Haurin, Hederschott and Ling, 1987).

2. **Race:** Race is also a factor in home ownership. However, Joseph Gyourko and Peter Linneman found that discrimination is not the cause of the impact of race on the investment decision. Rather, the cause is more likely associated with the increasing cost of housing (due to large downpayments, fees and zoning) and the inability of black households to meet the wealth constraint.

   This is related to the lack of intergenerational wealth transfers from their parents, transfers to which white households with similar characteristics may have access. Basically, suburban land use policies have raised the cost of home ownership and "disproportionately punished members of the middle class whose parents cannot transfer wealth for downpayments" (Gyourko and Linneman, 1995).

3. **Gender:** The gender of the head of the household is also important in home ownership. Males often have higher incomes which are more certain. Certainty of income is important with gender because males will, most likely, never leave the workforce for such expected events as child bearing and rearing. Following the same lines as the age factor, males have the opportunity to gain more experience in the workforce (by working continuously over their work life) and even more with a particular company. Therefore, males are more likely to at least maintain a certain level of income. Since males have these higher, more certain incomes, they are more likely to secure a loan or mortgage. Thus, males are more willing to commit to home ownership.

4. **Education:** The level of educational attainment also will determine the home ownership decision. An individual with a high level of educational attainment will often have a good job with a generous salary. A higher income provides an individual

with the funds to cover the initial costs incurred through home buying. Also, an individual with more education often saves more of his income which creates the capital and wealth to secure a loan.

Therefore, he has a greater ability to be approved for a mortgage. Because of this link between education, income and savings, an individual's educational attainment will influence his home ownership decision.

5. **Parental Home Ownership**: Whether or not the parents of an individual owned a house is important to the home ownership decision. First of all, children often look to their parents as financial examples. Parental tenure choice may condition the child's home ownership decision (DiSalvo and Ermisch, 1997). Second, parents who own homes often have a certain level of wealth which creates intergenerational transfers for their children- assets and wealth to pass down to future generations.

Individuals with lower levels of educational attainment and stagnant or declining real incomes often become home owners due to better access to intergenerational transfers from their parents (Gyourko and Linneman, 1995). Also, children of home owners are aware of the costs and benefits associated with home ownership and, thus, are more able to accurately assess the net benefits of home ownership. Therefore, if the parents own a home then their children also are more likely to own a home.

6. **Age:** Age is also a major determinant of home ownership for several reasons. First, older households have higher incomes. These households have spent more years in the workforce and their incomes have most likely risen with their level of experience. Older households are more financially prepared to cover the cost of a housing investment.

Older households also have more certainty of income. As a household gains increasingly more experience in the workforce or with a particular company, it is more likely that it will, at least, maintain a certain level of outcome. In other words, as a household's level of experience increases, it is less likely to lose its income altogether in the near future. Thus, older households are more likely to commit to home ownership. Also, older households have more wealth. This means that an investment in housing is more easily diversified and a smaller proportion of the wealth of older households contributes toward the housing investment. This leads to a preference for home ownership. Finally, older households are also less mobile - they tend to relocate less often than younger households.

Therefore, their annual-equivalent transaction costs are lower which makes home ownership more attractive (Cabrera, 2012)

It is important to realize that there is an offsetting effect. As an individual grows older, his prospective ownership life is shorter. This creates a shorter stream of benefits that potentially could be negative. However, older households may have the wealth to cover the initial cost of home ownership and obtain their desired level of net benefits.

7. **Marital Status:** The marital status of an individual will also affect home ownership. Married couples are often interested in "settling down" and are therefore less mobile than unmarried individuals.

Less mobility leads to lower annual-equivalent transaction costs in a housing purchase and likelihood of home ownership. Married couples also often pool their income and wealth. By pooling their income and wealth, they may be able to cross the wealth constraint that prevented home ownership as single individuals. Finally, married couples often forecast a future with children and will want to provide a stable environment to raise them. With more people in a household, the level of net benefits of home ownership increases. Hence, married couples are looking to make long term investment decisions with their money. With the equity and net benefits that home ownership provides, it is a smart investment decision. Therefore, if an individual is married, he has a greater probability of owning a home. Past studies have found that, with rising incomes, the impact of marital status is declining. Even so, it is still a strong influence in the home ownership decision (Gyourko and Linneman, 1995).

8. **Family Size:** The last factor in the home ownership decision is the size of a family. Past studies have found that the presence of a child in a household has a significant positive effect on home ownership, (Gyourko and Linneman, 1995) found a 20% increase in the probability for households with children compared to those without children. An increasing number of children yields a greater need for home ownership. In fact, buying a home may be less costly (with mortgage payments and tax benefits) than renting the space that would accommodate larger families. On the other hand, large families may be subject to financial constraints that may prevent home ownership. With more children in the family, the day-to-day expenses (food, day care, illnesses, etc.) increase drastically and may not allow for a sizeable commitment of income and wealth.

However, this study will follow the theory preferred in past studies which predicts a higher probability of ownership for households with children.

2.4 Homeownership

Carliner (1974), examines the underlying factors of homeownership. He proposes four factors affecting homeownership: household's income, relative price of rental versus homeownership, the stability of household demand for housing, and the type of house desired. This last factor includes the location of the house as on expression of desirability. Other variables included are age, size of family, type of family (single men, single women, married, divorced men, and divorced women), location (urban versus rural), race, and income. Carliner (1974) did not distinguish between permanent and current income. Using data from the 1967 Survey of Economic Opportunity (SEO) in the United States, he found that: as the age of the individual increases the likelihood of homeownership increases; larger families increase the probability of homeownership; married status increases the probability of ownership; rural locations increases the probability of homeownership; white households are more likely to be homeowners; and income positively increases homeownership probability.

Home ownership is a legal right to possession of a residence by a person, family or households. According to (Hulchanski, 2007), home ownership is characterized by housing ' tenure', and housing tenure can primarily be categorized into two (2); rental and owner occupier. Housing affordability on the other hand and according to Stone (2006) relates to individuals constituted as households in relation to their housing situation.

Home ownership of urban workforce housing in Nigeria has been on rental tenureship since in the 18th century during the colonial period, (Olotuah, 2009) until recently when government started changing its course to mortgage, and owner-occupier home ownership of the entire existing urban workforce housing in the country.

The current policy drive in the country is geared towards affordable housing delivery for home ownership in both owner-occupier and mortgage ownership. This is evident in the monetization process commenced in the year 2001 by the Federal government, with a policy drive in sales of houses to the workers in the public sector (i.e. the workforce) in Ahuja, which has also been spreading to some states within the country.

While the owner-occupier scheme that is tied to mortgage was observed to have low interest rate of not more than 5% and a considerable amortization period, the owner-occupier scheme based on monthly deduction from salary has a considerable level of subsidy, but with a short amortization period.

Ayedun and Oluwatobi (2011) asserted that lack of political will as well as inaccessibility to financial and other resources required for home provision has been a major impediment. Sequel to that, serious problem of inadequate home, resulting from many years of neglect, undeveloped housing finance system, limited supply of long term funds, high interest rate on mortgages, high cost of land and building materials, poor planning and implementation of housing policies and programmes, existence of administrative bottlenecks which make processing and securing of approval of building plans, Certificates of Occupancy and other necessary government permits very difficult and the unmitigated corruption in the allocation of government lands within the framework of the Land Use Act, Cap.202 LFN 1990 (Ogwu, 2006, Akomolede, 2007, and Onyike, 2007). The problem is further compounded by the high incidence of corruption in all other relevant sectors of the Nigerian economy and the lack of adequate political will by the government to deal decisively with the housing problem. There is also the problem of conflict of objectives among actors and stakeholders in the housing industry namely: the funding institutions and the developers on one side and the consumers of housing on the other side. Moreover, the profit maximization objective of the developers and funding institutions tends to cssonflict with the affordability of housing to the housing consumers especially the low-income earners (Draft National Housing Policy, 2004) with the government which is supposed to play active role at solving the accentuated problem of housing provision in the country standing by as a disinterested umpire.

An assessment of sustainable housing provision over the years in the country according to (Chukwujekwu, 2006), Housing provision is constrained by the under listed summarised problems which include but not limited to the following:

i. Escalating high cost of building materials.

ii. Inaccessibility to low and cheap housing finance for construction.

iii. Lack of rebate for importers of building materials.

iv. Poor remuneration and low minimum wage of workers resulting in low purchasing power that unattractive to developers.

v. Ineffective mortgage system to support purchasing power of low and middle income earners in the country.

vi. Lack of political will and commitment by successive governments in the country.

vii. Total withdrawal of some tiers of government in direct construction of houses.

viii. High profit driven attitude of private developers arising from high cost of funds.

ix. Lack of government support in terms of provision of infrastructural facilities to bring down high cost of housing construction.

x. Dependency on imported building materials which increases the overall cost of housing units.

xi. Non acceptance of local building materials and inadequate funding of research efforts of local building materials, and

xii. Indiscipline, corruption and overpricing of contract sums of housing projects.

To address the myriad problems confronting sustainable home provision in Nigeria, the following strategies are put forward which will go a long way in solving the problem of homes provision in Nigeria.

Ayedun and Oluwatobi (2011) highlighted and discussed some factors such as:

1. Building Materials

2. Land Tenure System

3. Housing Finance

1. Building materials

Building materials and components are import dependent and that makes them very expensive in the face of the value of the country's currency (Naira) and global inflation. With low earning capacity of majority of the country's citizens, the building materials are rendered out of their reach. It is regrettable to note that some traditional alternative building materials such as burnt or/and vibrated bricks and roof/ceiling tiles which are locally produced in the country but found no favour from average Nigerians and as such has not been popularised while their production costs are not competitive enough because of the problem associated with technology and economies of scale.

To solve the problem associated with high cost of building materials, readily available local building materials should be researched into with a view to improving their qualities and render them suitable for producing cost-effective, aesthetically attractive and durable houses. Such improved local materials will significantly reduce the cost of housing.

2. Land tenure system

Ironically, the national land policy, the Land Use Act which was promulgated in 1978 with the intention of making land readily available and accessible to all eligible Nigerians, has ended up constituting itself into clog in the wheel of housing provision in the country. The Land Use Act was promulgated with the intention of streamlining the land tenure systems in the country by vesting the ownership and title to all lands in the country on the Governors of the respective states of the Federation for the purpose of easy management and accessibility by those interested in the acquisition of lands in the country. However, the contentious issues of Governor's consent for any subsequent transaction in land and the intractable government bureaucracy and bottlenecks have made the procurement of land problematic, unnecessarily expensive and out rightly out of the reach of most of Nigerians citizens most especially in the urban centres of the country. To the average citizens of the country, the government is a distant phenomenon, very much out of their reach, their inability to procure land automatically translate to the fact that they cannot be seen to make any effort to build or construct houses of their own even on self-help basis.

3. Housing finance

In many parts of the world, most especially the developed countries, the sources of housing finance is from government, individual savings, life insurance reserves, commercial banks, savings and loans institutions (Primary Mortgage Institutions or Building Societies), However, in Nigeria the main sources of housing finance are Government- by way of loans staff to build their houses, grants to the Federal Housing Authority by the Federal Government and various State Housing corporations by the State Governments as well as through individual savings. Private enterprise has played a major role in providing finance for housing in the country. The bulk of housing stock in the country are constructed through individual efforts.

The commercial banks and insurance companies have not play significant role in housing provision efforts in the country. Commercial banking practices does not give room for long term lending which housing construction require. Whereas in United Kingdom and most countries in Europe, commercial banks and insurance companies very readily lend money for home ownership. In Nigeria, the lending policy of insurance companies are very conservative while commercial banks by nature of their operations find it difficult giving loans for projects with long gestation period which is the hallmark of housing construction.

If more houses are to be built and less dependence placed on the resources of government only, then there is the necessity of finding new sources of money for housing construction. There is need for total overhauling of the county's mortgage system with a very to making it relevant to the country's housing industry. At moment, operations most of the Primary Mortgage Institutions operating in the country are not too different from that of commercial banks. Moreover, their capital base is too weak to support the requirements of prospective borrowers for housing construction.

According to, Nwakanma and Nnamdi (2013), assimilated or integrated households are more likely to own a house than those separated or marginalized. Thus, the probable determinants of homeownership as identified in various literatures include; Employment status; Income; Education; Marital status; Family composition; Access to Home financing; Discrimination etc.

In another study in Nigeria, Onyike (2009) examined the affordability of housing by public servants in owerri city in Nigeria, under the new salaries and allowances regime, he considered a market value survey of 66 bungalows and houses, he found out that only those on salary grade levels 13 and above in the federal public service and grade levels 16 and above in the Imo state civil service can afford the cheapest adequate bungalows in owerri at 6% interest rate. At 18% interest rate only those on grade level 17 and above in the federal service and none in the Imo state service can afford adequate housing. In his conclusion, majority of public servants cannot afford adequate housing without substantial assistance.

Haurin and Lee (1989), motivated their study of the length of stay in a particular dwelling by noting that the user cost of ownership depends on the duration of stay in a home. Using Panel Study of Income Dynamics (PSID) data, they estimated a length of stay equation; however, they did not include race as an explanatory variable.

Henderson and Ioannides (1989), also estimated the duration of stay in a dwelling with PSID data, using a failure time (duration) econometric model. Their estimation method accounted for incomplete spells (censoring), these occurring when a survey ends prior to a household's departure from a dwelling unit. Also, they estimated separate duration equations for owners and renters. For owners, Henderson and Ioannides (1989), found that increased education reduces the length of stay, but the effect diminishes for older households. The duration of stay fell with increased age of head until owners reached age 61. The length of stay as an owner for White household heads was longer than that of all other minority groups, but this racial difference was not present for renters. Marginally significant to the explanation of owners' duration of stay was marital status, but surprisingly being married reduced the length of stay. Also marginally significant with a negative effect was household wealth, but the size of impact diminished with age.

Gronberg and Reed (1992) continued this strand of research, but they used American Housing Survey (AHS) data. For homeowners, they found that length of stay in a dwelling is shorter for households with greater income, which is consistent with Henderson and Ioannides' finding for wealth. Length of stay for owners is shorter as education and age increase, if the individual is married, and for larger families. For renters, the effect of marriage, education, and family size are the same as for owners, but those of age and income are the opposite.

30

A different perspective on homeowners' length of stay comes from the literature that links mobility and various lock-in effects with homeownership. Stein (1995) argued that homeowners may delay the sale of their home if falling house prices result in low or negative home equity (house price lock-in). If the household moved, it might not be able to make the required down payment on another dwelling. Henley (1998) examines the mobility of British homeowners and finds that negative home equity significantly reduces the probability of a move and thus it extends the duration of stay.

According to Haughwout & Peach (2009), discussed and enumerated some benefits of homeownership.

They further state that the case for government support for homeownership rests in large part on the view that ownership is an effective mechanism for aligning incentives such that economically efficient actions are taken. Because owners have a financial interest in the property, they have incentives to take actions that will maintain or increase its value. Some of these actions, like fixing a leaky roof, are closely related to the house itself. Others, like investing resources in the betterment of the neighborhood and the community, create what economists call "positive externalities" because they have beneficial effects more generally in the local area. Owners may take these actions because they have an equity stake in the house and therefore in the community.

Homeowners, unlike renters, typically receive 100 percent of any increase or decrease in the value of the houses they are living in. This creates incentives for homeowners to act in an economically efficient manner since their actions are reflected – or "capitalized"– in their home prices. Fischel (2001) calls this the "home voter hypothesis." These capitalization effects have been empirically documented along a number of dimensions. Holding constant the tax costs of publicly supported education, houses located in school districts that provide better educational outcomes sell at a premium (Black (1999), Barrow & Rouse (2004)).4

Capitalization can also lead to lower house prices. Localities where public sector unions appear to have negotiated large wage tend to have lower house values (Gyourko & Tracy (1989). The fact that these community-level characteristics affect house prices provides incentives for homeowners to support efficient public policies and projects in much the same way a corporation's shareholders will support private projects that have a positive net present value for the firm. In the case of rental properties (or negative equity homeowners), the landlord (or lender) receives the benefits of gains in asset values up to the value of the mortgage. In both cases, an agency problem arises from the fact that the beneficiary of gains in the value of the house accrue to someone other than the occupant of the house, who is the one in a position to take actions to maximize this value through maintenance, public participation, etc.

Is there evidence that supports the home voter hypothesis – that is, that capitalization effects actually induce homeowners to act in the best interests of the property and the community? Maintenance and repair is an important offset to the depreciation of a house over time. The typical homeowner expends several thousand dollars a year in maintenance (Gyourko & Tracy (2006), Harding *et al* (2007)). Before the current housing crisis, relatively few households ever found themselves in a "negative equity" position – that is, where the current value of the house is less than the mortgage balance. However, there have been regional house price cycles that have allowed researchers to study the effect of negative equity on homeowner behavior. Gyourko and Saiz (2004) document that homeowners in negative equity situations tend to under maintain their property relative to other homeowners. Also consistent with the home voter hypothesis, researchers have found that elderly households without school age children still support local education bond issues. While altruism could be a factor, the most likely explanation appears to be the belief that supporting local schools will improve the value of their houses (Bergstrom *et al* (1982), Hilber & Mayer (2009)). Green and White (1997) find that children of homeowners are more likely to finish school and less likely to have children as teenagers than children of renters. Finally, homeowners have a higher voting rate in local elections and are more aware of local issues and the identities of state and local civic leaders (see DiPasquale & Glaeser (1999)), while these studies all point in the direction of social benefits from homeownership, it is important to point out that other research is far less conclusive. Recent work by Engelhardt *et al* (2009) indicates that the measured benefits from homeownership may result from the fact that people who choose to buy homes are different from those who choose to rent, in that they are also more likely to value investing in social capital. They conclude, for example, that the estimates described above "overstate the impact of homeownership on political involvement and that the true effect is zero or negative," at least for their small sample of low-income households. While more research is warranted here, existing public support for homeownership implies that policymakers believe that its social benefits are substantial.

Gandelman (2005) discussed on homeownership and gender and opines that there is a large literature on the analysis of housing tenure choice. One dimension that has been often incorporated into the empirical analysis is whether the household head is a man or a woman. Surprisingly, very few authors comment on their results of household headship. In this paper, we argue that the determinants of women household headship and those of homeownership are correlated and therefore the specification used in most studies has an endogeneity problem that leads to inconsistent and often counterintuitive results. If women's marital status is not exogenous to the tenure choice, then, even in the presence of discrimination against women in the housing markets, a naive view of the data may reflect that women headed households have higher probabilities of owning their home. For instance, those women that do not have a place where to live, have lower income, have more children, etc. will probably not divorce their husbands even if they want to. Therefore, there is a selection bias in which woman headed families tend to have better socioeconomic indicators than what they would have if woman headship were a completely exogenous process.

Hassan (2005) talked about homeownership through mortgage finance and says, in recent years, all over the world, considerable effort has been made to extend opportunities to mortgages so that ordinary people can own their own homes. This is the product of two related factors: On the one hand, the housing finance market has become more competitive as new providers have been encouraged to enter the market. Such providers have been seeking new customers to extend their activities. Thus, the extension of mortgage services is a commercial response to market conditions. On the other hand, the state has been looking to the market to address housing need. Faced with considerable housing problems and seeking to reduce public expenditure, governments have sought to encourage the market to address needs where possible.

After explicitly reviewing the necessary literatures on homeownership, a gap that is yet to be filled was detected, and the gap is factors influencing homeownership, especially in the Ibadan metropolis of Oyo State.

CHAPTER THREE

RESEARCH METHODOLOGY

3.1 Introduction

In the preceding chapters, an attempt was made to lay a foundation for this study. The aim, objectives, and important of the study were well explained in the first chapter while the second chapter focused researchers view on factors influencing homeownership. This chapter discusses the methodology used in this research including research design, sampling frame, sampling techniques, sampling size, research analytical tool, data types and sources and procedures for data collections.

3.2 Research design

Research design entails the plan, arrangement, structure and strategy of investigation conceived to obtain answers to research questions in order to control variance or deviation and to suggest adequate observation of the study area and a proper means to analyze the data obtained from the questionnaire administered. It also explains the procedure the research will follow in arriving at the result; means of data presentation and details on steps taken to achieve the objectives of the research work. This research work is designed to acquire data from primary data for analysis and presentation.

3.3 Study population

Population is a collection of individual items whether of people or things that is to be observed in a given situation. The respondents to be administered questionnaires for the purpose of this study are civil servants in Ibadan metropolis.

3.4 Sample frame

The sample frame for this research work are the civil servants in Ibadan metropolis The sample frame will be limited Oyo State government ministries workers in the area of case study, the sample frame for the Ministry of Establishment and Training is 145, Ministry of Local Government and Chieftaincy Matters is 89, Ministry of Land, Housing and Survey is 205, Ministry of Youth and Sport is 250 and Ministry of Physical Planning and Development Unit is 60, All totaling 749. And this research will be limited to these five (5) Ministries because of availability and accessibility of data on other Ministries.

3.5 Sample size

This is usually considered when the size of the sample frame is large. It aimed at determining the working population that will be used for this study. The adoption of sample size is to allow the researcher to be able to have a better coverage of the study area.

For purposes of achieving the study's objectives, this research will focus on 15% each from the Ministry of Establishment and Training, Ministry of Local Government and Chieftaincy Matters, Ministry of Land, Housing and Survey is, Ministry of Youth and Sport and Ministry of Physical Planning and Development Unit, 15% of the five (5) Ministries is 113, thus the sample size is 113. The questionnaires will be administered to ensure and achieve maximum response.

3.6 Method of sampling

A sample is a part of population observed for the purpose of making scientific statement or taking a decision about the population. A sample can be random, systematic, stratified, cluster sampling.

And for the purpose of this research the systematic sampling will be adopted

Systematic sampling

Systematic sampling relies on arranging the target population according to some ordering scheme and then selecting elements at regular intervals through that ordered list. Systematic sampling involves a random start and then proceeds with the selection of every nth element from then onwards. In this case, $n=$ (population size/sample size). It is important that the starting point is not automatically the first in the list, but is instead randomly chosen from within the first to the nth element in the list. A simple example would be to select every 15th name from the telephone directory.

3.7 Instruments of data collection

These are the fact finding strategies, they are the tools for data collection, and they include Questionnaire, Interview, Observation and Reading. Essentially the researcher must ensure that the instrument chosen is valid and reliable. The validity and reliability of any research project depends to a large extent on the appropriateness of the instruments. Whatever procedure one uses to collect data, it must be critically examined to check the extent to which it is likely to give you the expected results.

For the purpose of this study, the questionnaire mode of data collection will be adopted.

3.8 Questionnaire design

This is a way of collecting information whereby questions are designed in order to get responses that help in achieving the aim and objectives of the research work. These questions can be in form of structured or unstructured format.

1. This is a data collection instrument mostly used in normative surveys. This is a systematically prepared form   or document with a set of questions deliberately designed to elicit responses from respondents or research informants for the purpose of collecting data or information.

2. It is a form of inquiry document, which contains a systematically compiled and well organised series of questions intended to elicit the information which will provide insight into the nature of the problem under study.

3. It is a form that contains a set of questions on a topic or group of topics designed to be answered by the respondent.

4. The respondents are the population samples of the study. The answers provided by the respondents constitute the data for the research.

Types of Questionnaires

1. Structured or closed form

2. Unstructured, open ended form

1. Structured questionnaires

They are those in which some control or guidance is given for the answer. This may be described as closed form because the questions are basically short, requiring the respondent to provide a 'yes' or 'no' response, or checking an item out of a list of given responses. Questions that require yes or no answers are also termed as Dichotomous questions. It may, also be multiple choice options from which the respondent selects the answer closer to their own opinion. The respondent's choices are limited to the set of options provided.

2. Unstructured questionnaire

This type which is also termed as open-ended or unrestricted type of questionnaire calls for a free response in the respondent's own words. The respondent frames and supplies the answer to the question raised in the questionnaire. It also constitute questions which give the

38

respondent an opportunity to express his or her opinions from a set of options. Spaces are often provided for respondents to make their inputs.

The questionnaire will be prepared and administered to Oyo State government secretariat workers in the study area. These questionnaires will be answered by the respondents, analysed and then interpreted so as to reach a reasonable conclusion with a view to give proper recommendation.

3.9 Data analysis and presentation

Research generally, is meant to generate data for analysis and this result in a large volume of statistical information which is mostly in its raw stage. In order to use data for the objectives of a research, they have to be reduced to manageable dimensions.

The data gathered will be analyzed using descriptive statistics involving the use of percentage and weighted mean analysis, the result are presented in form of frequency tables and Relative importance index (RII), and the data obtained was ranked on a 5 point Likert Scale using relative importance index to give a clearer picture of the results obtained from the field survey.

CHAPTER FOUR

DATA ANALYSIS AND DISCUSSION OF FINDINGS

4.1 Introduction

This chapter deals with the presentation, analysis and interpretation of data collected in response to the questionnaires administered to civil servants in Ibadan metropolis. A total of one hundred and thirteen (113) questionnaires were administered on civil servants out of 749 staffs in the sampled ministries.

The 113 questionnaires was arrived at by taking 15% of the staff capacity of each of the sampled ministries in the Oyo State government secretariat , Ibadan, Oyo State, Out of this number, ninety-five (95) valid questionnaires were retrieved and used for the analysis, indicating a response rate of (84.07%). A systematic sampling method was used to collect the data. Data collected were analyzed using the SPSS version 17 software. The descriptive statistics of the socio-economic characteristics of the civil servants were presented and analyzed using frequencies and percentages. The housing preferences of homeownership were analyzed using weighted mean analysis.

The factors influencing homeownership were analyzed using weighted mean analysis.

4.2 Socio-Economic Characteristics of Respondents

This sub-chapter of the research work as to do with some factors which were extracted from the research work and analysed.

Table 1. Distribution of Respondents according to Ministries

	Name	Frequency	Percent
1.	Ministry of Land, Housing and surveying	25	26.3
2.	Ministry of Physical Planning and Urban Development	9	9.5
3.	Ministry of Youth and Sport	31	32.6
4.	Ministry of Chieftaincy and local government matters	13	13.7
5.	Ministry of Establishment and Training	17	17.9
Total		95	100.0

Source: Author's field work, 2016.

Table 1 above presents the numbers of civil servants in the sampled ministries. The result reveals that the 'Ministry of Establishment and Training' is 17.9%, 'Ministry of Local Government and Chieftaincy Matters' is 13.7%, 'Ministry of Land, Housing and Survey' is 26.3%, 'Ministry of Youth and Sport' is 36.2% and 'Ministry of Physical Planning and Development Unit' is 9.5% of the total respondents surveyed.

Table 2. Distribution of civil servants according to Number of years in service

The table below shows the range of the years in service of civil servants in the sampled ministries.

S/N	Range	Frequency	Percent
1.	1-5 years	10	10.5
2.	6-10 years	31	32.6
3.	11-15 years	33	34.7
4.	16-20 years	3	3.2
5.	21years and above	18	18.9
	Total	95	100.0

Source: Author's field work, 2016.

Table 2 above presents the survey data on the number of years in service of respondents surveyed. The result reveals the percentage of those that been in service for '1-5 years' is 10.5%, '6-10 years' is 36.2%, '11-15 years' is 34.7%, '16-20 years' is 3.2% and '21 and above' is 18.9% of the total respondents surveyed, the highest age range of civil servants which was 11-15 years in service shows that the results or recommendations of this research takes into cognizance civil servants with longer years of service and hence, it considered those with more longer years in service.

Table 3. Distribution of Respondents according to the status of civil servants

The table below show the status of civil servants that were sampled.

	Frequency	Percent
1. Junior staffs	52	54.7
2. Senior staffs	43	45.3
Total	95	100.0

Source: Author's field work, 2016.

Table 3 above presents the survey data on status of respondents surveyed. The result reveals that the percentage 'junior staffs' is 54.7% and 'senior staff' is 45.3% of the total respondents surveyed, a larger percentage of the respondents are junior staffs and this reveal that there are more of junior staffs than senior staffs amongst civil servants in the sampled ministries, and most of the senior staffs cannot be easily accessed.

Table 4. Distribution of Respondents according to the age range of civil servants

The table below shows the age range of civil servants in the surveyed ministries.

Age range	Frequency	Percent
1. Below 20 years	1	1.1
2. 21-30 years	28	29.5
3. 31-40 years	35	36.8
4. 41-50 years	25	26.3
5. 51 years and above	6	6.3
Total	95	100.0

Source: Author's field work, 2016.

Table 4 above presents the survey data on the age distribution of respondents surveyed. The result reveals that the percentage of those ''below 20 years'' is 1.1%, '21-30 years' is 29.5%, '31-40 years' is 36.8%, '41-50 years' is 26.3%, '51 years and above' is 6.3% of the total respondents surveyed, the age range of civil servants that participated most in the research was 31- 40 years, and this indicate that the housing preferences of these persons are modern because they are mostly youths and youths will prefer a modern home.

Table 5. Distribution of Respondents according to the gender of civil servants

Gender	Frequency	Percent
1. Male	41	43.2
2. Female	54	56.8
Total	95	100.0

Source: Author's field work, 2016.

Table 5 above presents the survey data on the gender distribution of respondents surveyed. The result reveals that the percentage of the 'Male' is 43.2% and 'Female' is 56.8% of the total respondents surveyed, this result shows that there more of female than male amongst civil servants, and this majorly because most of the clerical office works are preferably handled by female.

Table 6. Distribution of Respondents according to the marital status of civil servants

status	Frequency	Percent
1. Single	24	25.3
2. Married	71	74.7
Total	95	100.0

Source: Author's field work, 2016.

Table 6 above presents the survey data on the marital distribution of respondents surveyed. The result reveals that the percentage of the 'Single' is 25.3% and 'Married' is 74.7% of the total respondents surveyed, the percentage of civil servants that are married are more than the singles and this is evident of the fact that most the civil servants in the sampled ministries.

Table 7. Distribution of Respondents according to the academic qualification of civil servants in the sampled ministries

Qualification	Frequency	Percent
1. National Diploma	45	47.4
2. Higher National Diploma	28	29.5
3. Bachelor of Science	15	15.8
4. Master of Science	4	4.2
5. Others	3	3.2
Total	95	100.0

Source: Author's field work, 2016.

Table 7 above presents the survey data on the academic qualification of respondents surveyed. The result reveals that the percentage of those with 'National Diploma' is 47.4%,'Higher National Diploma' is 29.5%, 'Bachelor of Science' is 15.8%, 'Master of

Science' is 4.2%, and 'others' is 3.2%, of the total respondents surveyed, the academic qualification of the civil servants with the highest frequency was 'National Diploma' and this because the minimum criteria of civil servants for recruitments are open to all and it will help reduce the wage bill of government than employing staffs with higher qualification since most of their duties are clerical in nature.

Table 8. Distribution of Respondents according to the salary range of civil servants

Range	Frequency	Percent
1. 31,000-50,000 Naira	37	38.9
2. 51,000-70,000 Naira	17	17.9
3. 71,000-90,000 Naira	27	28.4
4. 91,000 Naira and above	14	14.7
Total	95	100.0

Source: Author's field work, 2016.

Table 8 above presents the survey data on the salary distribution of respondents surveyed. The result reveals that the percentage of the '₦31, 000-₦50, 000' is 39.8%, '₦51, 000-₦70, 000' is 17.9%, '₦71, 000-₦90, 000' is 28.4%, '₦91, 000 and above' is 14.7% of the total respondents surveyed, the salary range with the highest frequency is ₦31,000-₦50,000 and this is because there are more junior staffs with relatively lower level than senior staffs and this in turn will affect their savings.

Table 9. Distribution of Respondents according to the Family size of civil servants in the sampled ministries

	Frequency	Percent
1. 1-2	25	26.3
2. 3-4	51	53.7
3. 5-6	19	20.0
Total	95	100.0

Source: Author's field work, 2016.

Table 9 above presents the survey data on the family size distribution of respondents surveyed. The result reveals that the percentage of the '1 -2' is 26.3%, '3 -4'is 53.7%, and '5 -6'is 20.0% of the total respondents surveyed, the family size range with the highest range was 3- 4, this shows the most of the civil servants are married with an average of two kids.

4.3 Housing preferences of the civil servants

This section assessed the housing preferences of the civil servants by rating the importance of the preferences as perceived by the respondents. In order to ascertain the respondents' views on housing preferences amongst the respondents in the study area, respondents were allowed to express their view on different housing preferences. To do this, different housing preferences were identified. Each of the preferences were rated using the five point Likert scale of "Highly preferred", "Preferred", "Somewhat preferred", "Not preferred", and "Not at all preferred". To arrive at the respondents aggregated view on each preference, each of the rating above was assigned value of 5, 4, 3, 2 and 1 respectively. The Total Weight Value (TWV) for each view is obtained through the summation of the product of the number of responses for each rating and the respective weight value. This is expressed

mathematically as:

$$TWV = \sum_{I=5}^{1} XiYi$$

Where: TWV = Total Weight Value

Xi= number of residents to rate an attribute i; and

Yi= the weight assigned a value (i = 5, 4, 3, 2, 1).

The respondents' aggregated view on each of the factor was arrived at by dividing TWV by

the summation of the residents to each of the five ratings. The analysis of the responses

evolved into an index called, *"RPI- Relative Preferences Index"* (*RPI*) which can take the

value between 1 and 5.

4.3.1 Civil servants Preferences Index for the ministry of establishment and training

Table 10. **Respondents Preferences Index for the ministry of establishment and training**

S/N	Preferences	HP	P	SWP	NP	NAP	TWV	(RPI)	RANK
1	Bungalow	7	8	1	-	-	70	4.38	1
2	Detached house	5	9	1	-	-	64	4.27	3
3	Semi-detached	4	10	2	-	-	66	4.13	6
4	Terrace house	2	5	9	-	-	57	3.56	7
5	Tenement house	1	1	14	-	-	51	3.19	8
6	Duplex	10	13	1	-	1	106	4.25	5
7	Condominium	8	4	3	-	-	65	4.33	2
8	Flat house	8	5	1	-	1	64	4.27	3
9	Row house	1	1	3	-	11	29	1.81	9
10	Others	-	-	-	-	-	-	-	
	Mean of $\sum$RPI = 34.11/9 = 3.79								

Key: *HP- Highly preferred, P-Preferred, SWP- Somewhat preferred, NP- Not preferred,*
NAP- Not at all preferred, TWV-Total Weighted Value, RPI- **Relative Preference Index,**
ministry of establishment and training.
Source: Author's field work, 2016.

48

As indicated in the table above, Bungalow was ranked first with **RPI** of 4.38 amongst

the preferences, and this is because of the civil servants salary, family and level of education.

Condominium was ranked second with **RPI** of 4.33, Flat and Detached house were ranked

third with **RPI** of 4.27, Duplex was ranked fifth with **RPI** of 4.25, Semi-detached was ranked

sixth with **RPI** of 4.13, Terrace house was ranked seventh with **RPI** of 3.56, Tenement house

was ranked eighth with **RPI** of 3.19, Row house was ranked ninth with **RPI** of 1.81.

4.3.2 Civil servants Preferences Index for the ministry of physical planning and development unit

Table 11. **Civil servants Preferences Index for the ministry of physical planning and development unit**

S/N	Preferences	HP	P	SWP	NP	NAP	TWV	(RPI)	RANK
1	Bungalow	3	6	-	-	-	39	4.33	2
2	Detached house	3	6	-	-	-	39	4.33	2
3	Semi-detached	-	8	1	-	-	35	3.89	5
4	Terrace house	1	2	5	1	-	30	3.33	7
5	Tenement house	2	1	4	1	1	29	3.22	8
6	Duplex	3	2	4	-	-	35	3.89	5
7	Condominium	5	1	2	-	1	36	4.00	4
8	Flat house	6	1	2	-	-	40	4.44	1
9	Row house	1	-	5	-	3	23	2.56	9
10	Others	-	-	-	-	-	-	-	
	Mean of $\sum$RPI = 51.03/9 = 5.67								

Key: *HP- Highly preferred, P-Preferred, SWP- Somewhat preferred, NP- Not preferred,*
NAP- Not at all preferred , TWV-Total Weighted Value, RPI- Relative Preferences Index,
ministry of physical planning and development unit.
Source: Author's field work, 2016.

As indicated in the table below, Flat was ranked first with **RPI** of 4.44 amongst the

preference, why Flat house was preferred here was because it will serve as an alternative

means of income and civil servants with bigger family size. Bungalow and Detached house were ranked second with **RPI** of 4.33, Condominium was ranked fourth with **RPI** of 4.00,

Duplex and Semi-detached were ranked fifth with **RPI** of 3.89, Terrace house was ranked

seventh with **RPI** of 3.33, Tenement house was ranked eighth with **RPI** of 3.22, Row house

was ranked ninth with **RPI** of 2.56.

4.3.3 Civil servants Preferences Index for the ministry of Land, housing and survey

Table 12. **Civil servants Preferences Index for the ministry of Land, housing and survey**

S/N	Preferences	HP	P	SWP	NP	NAP	TWV	(RPI)	RANK
1	Bungalow	6	17	2	-	-	104	4.16	5
2	Detached house	5	15	1	1	2	92	3.83	6
3	Semi-detached	4	10	6	1	2	82	3.57	7
4	Terrace house	2	7	11	1	2	75	3.26	8
5	Tenement house	1	9	10	1	2	75	3.26	8
6	Duplex	14	6	4	-	1	107	4.28	4
7	Condominium	14	5	3	1	-	101	4.39	2
8	Flat house	14	10	-	-	-	110	4.58	1
9	Row house	5	2	3	1	11	99	4.30	3
10	Others								
	Mean of $\sum$RPI = 32.64/9 = 3.96								

Key *HP- Highly preferred, P-Preferred, SWP- Somewhat preferred, NP- Not preferred,
NAP- Not at all preferred, TWV-Total Weighted Value, RII- Relative Preferences Index,*
ministry of Land, housing and survey.
Source: Author's field work, 2016.

As indicated in the table above, Flat house was ranked first with **RPI** of 4.58 amongst

the preference, the reason why Flat house was preferred here was because it will serve as an

alternative means of income and civil servants with bigger family size Condominium was

ranked second with **RPI** of 4.39, Row house was ranked third with **RPI** of 4.30, Duplex was

ranked fourth with **RPI** of 4.28, Bungalow was ranked fifth with **RPI** of 4.16, Detached house was ranked sixth with **RPI** of 3.83, Semi-detached was ranked seventh with **RPI** of 3.57, Terrace house and Tenement were ranked eighth with **RPI** of 3.26.

4.3.4 Civil servants Preferences Index for the ministry of Local government and chieftaincy matter

Table 13. **Civil servants Preferences Index for the ministry of Local government and chieftaincy matter**

S/N	Preferences	HP	P	SWP	NP	NAP	TWV	(RPI)	RANK
1	Bungalow	3	7	2	1	-	51	3.92	3
2	Detached house	2	6	4	1	-	48	3.69	5
3	Semi-detached	1	5	5	1	1	43	3.31	6
4	Terrace house	-	3	8	1	1	39	3.00	8
5	Tenement house	1	2	9	1	-	42	3.23	7
6	Duplex	9	1	2	-	-	55	4.58	1
7	Condominium	5	4	2	-	2	49	3.77	4
8	Flat house	8	3	-	1	1	55	4.23	2
9	Row house	1	-	1	1	9	19	1.58	9
10	Others								
	Mean of $\sum$**RPI = 31.31/9 = 3.48**								

Key: *HP- Highly preferred, P-Preferred, SWP- Somewhat preferred, NP- Not preferred, NAP- Not at all preferred, TWV-Total Weighted Value, RPI-* **Relative Preferences Index, ministry of Local government and chieftaincy matter.**
Source: Author's field work, 2016.

As indicated in the table above, Duplex was ranked first with **RPI** of 4.58 amongst the preferences, this may be as a result of the taste and family size of the civil servants. Flat was ranked second with **RPI** of 4.23, Bungalow was ranked third with **RPI** of 3.92, Condominium was ranked fourth with **RPI** of 3.77, Detached house were ranked fifth with **RPI** of 3.92, Semi-detached was ranked sixth with **RPI** of 3.31, Tenement was ranked seventh with **RPI** of 3.23, Terrace house was ranked eighth with **RPI** of 3.00, Row was ranked ninth with **RPI** of 1.58.

4.3.5 Civil servants Preferences Index for the ministry of youths and sport

Table 14. **Civil servants Preferences Index for the ministry of youths and sport**

S/N	Preferences	HP	P	SWP	NP	NAP	TWV	(RPI)	RANK
1	Bungalow	13	11	7	-	-	130	4.19	3
2	Detached house	7	15	8	1	-	121	3.90	4
3	Semi-detached	6	9	15	-	1	112	3.61	6
4	Terrace house	1	4	25	-	1	97	3.13	8
5	Tenement house	1	4	23	-	1	91	3.14	7
6	Duplex	25	3	3	-	-	146	4.71	1
7	Condominium	7	16	4	-	3	114	3.80	5
8	Flat house	22	4	3	-	2	137	4.42	2
9	Row house	-	-	1	5	19	32	1.28	9
10	Others	-	-	-	-	-	-	-	
	Mean of $\sum$**RPI = 32.22/9 = 3.58**								

Key: *HP- Highly preferred, P-Preferred, SWP- Somewhat preferred, NP- Not preferred, NAP- Not at all preferred, TWV-Total Weighted Value, RPI-* **Relative Preferences Index, ministry of youths and sport.**
Source: Author's field work, 2016.

As indicated in the table above, Duplex was ranked first with **RPI** of 4.71 amongst the factors, this may be as a result of the taste and family size of the civil servants. Flat was ranked second with **RPI** of 4.42, Bungalow was ranked third with **RPI** of 4.19, Detached house was ranked fourth with **RPI** of 3.90, Condominium was ranked fifth with **RPI** of 3.80, Semi-detached was ranked sixth with **RPI** of 3.61, Tenement was ranked seventh with **RPI** of 3.14, Terrace house was ranked eighth with **RPI** of 3.13, Row house was ranked ninth with **RPI** of 1.28.

4.3.6 Civil servants Preferences Index for the five (5) ministries

Table 15. Civil servants Preferences Index for the five (5) ministries

S/N	Preferences	HP	P	SWP	NP	NAP	TWV	(RPI)	RANK
1	Bungalow	32	50	12	1	-	398	4.19	5
2	Detached house	21	52	14	3	2	407	4.38	4
3	Semi-detached	15	41	30	2	4	337	3.66	6
4	Terrace house	6	21	58	3	4	298	3.24	7
5	Tenement house	6	16	60	3	4	284	3.19	8
6	Duplex	61	14	15	-	2	463	4.97	1
7	Condominium	39	29	14	1	6	416	4.62	2
8	Flat house	59	23	6	1	4	411	4.42	3
9	Row house	8	2	12	7	54	200	2.35	9
10	Others	-	-	-	-	-	-	-	
	Mean of $\sum$RPI = 35.01/9 = 3.89								

Key: : HP- Highly preferred, P-Preferred, SWP- Somewhat preferred, NP- Not preferred, NAP- Not at all preferred, TWV-Total Weighted Value, RPI- Relative Preferences Index, the five (5) ministries.
Source: Author's field work, 2016.

As indicated in the table above, Duplex was ranked first with **RPI** of 4.97 amongst the preferences, this may be as a result of the taste and family size of the civil servants. Condominium was ranked second with **RPI** of 4.62, Flat was ranked third with **RPI** of 4.42, Detached house was ranked fourth with **RPI** of 4.38, Bungalow was ranked fifth with **RPI** of 4.19, Semi-detached was ranked sixth with **RPI** of 3.66, Terrace house was ranked seventh **RPI** of 3.24, Tenement house was ranked eighth with **RPI** of 3.19, Row house was ranked ninth with **RPI** of 2.35.

4.4 Factors influencing homeownership in the study area

This section assessed the factors influencing homeownership of civil servants in the study area by rating the importance of the factors as perceived by the respondent. In order to ascertain the respondents' views on factors influencing homeownership amongst the respondents in the study area, respondents were allowed to express their view on different factors influencing homeownership. To do this, different influencing factors were identified. Each of the factors were rated using the five point Likert scale of "Very influential", "Influential", "Somewhat influential", "Not influential", and "Not at all influential". To arrive at the respondents aggregated view on each factor, each of the rating above was assigned value of 5, 4, 3, 2 and 1 respectively. The Total Weight Value (TWV) for each view is obtained through the summation of the product of the number of responses for each rating and the respective weight value. This is expressed mathematically as:

$$TWV = \sum_{i=5}^{1} X_i Y_i$$

Where: TWV = Total Weight Value

Xi= number of residents to rate an attribute i; and

Yi= the weight assigned a value (i = 5, 4, 3, 2, 1).

The respondents' aggregated view on each of the factor was arrived at by dividing TWV by the summation of the residents to each of the five ratings. The analysis of the responses evolved into an index called, *"RII- Relative Important of Index"* (*RII*) which can take the value between 1 and 5.

4.4.1 Civil servants Importance Index for the ministry of establishment and training

Table 16. **Civil servants Importance Index for the ministry of establishment and training**

S/N	Factors	VI	I	SWI	NI	NAI	TWV	(RII)	RANK
1	Salary	7	9	-	-	-	71	4.44	1
2	Marital status	-	12	4	-	-	60	3.75	5
3	Parental home ownership	3	4	8	-	1	56	3.50	9
4	Tribe	-	7	9	-	-	55	3.44	10
5	Gender	-	4	12	-	-	52	3.25	12
6	Education	-	3	11	1	1	48	3.00	14
7	Age	-	4	10	-	1	47	3.13	13
8	Land acquisition	3	7	4	-	1	56	3.73	7
9	Land security	2	9	4	-	1	59	3.68	8
10	Family size	1	5	9	-	1	53	3.31	11
11	Loan facilities	3	9	3	-	1	61	3.81	4
12	Lending rate	3	8	4	-	1	60	3.75	5
13	Costs of building materials	11	1	2	-	1	66	4.40	2
14	Personal priority	7	5	1	-	2	60	4.00	3
15	Others	-	-	-	-	-	-	-	

Mean of $\sum$RII = 51.24/14 = 3.66

Key: *VI- Very influential, I-Influential, SWI- Somewhat influential, NI- Not Influential,*
NAI- Not at all influential, TWV-Total Weighted Value, RII- **Relative Importance Index,**
ministry of establishment and training.
Source: Author's field work, 2016.

As indicated in the table above, Salary was ranked first with **RII** of 4.44 amongst the factors, this reveals that salary is a major determinant for civil servants to own a home and the higher their salary, the higher their savings which boost their chance of owning a home.

Costs of building materials was ranked second with **RII** of 4.40, Personal priority was ranked third with **RII** of 4.00, Loan facilities was ranked fourth with **RII** of 3.81, Lending rate and Marital status was ranked fifth with **RII** of 3.75, Land acquisition was ranked seventh with **RII** of 3.73, Land security was ranked eighth with **RII** of 3.68, Parental home ownership was ranked ninth with **RII** of 3.50, Tribe was ranked tenth with **RII** of 3.44 , Family size was ranked eleventh with **RII** of 3.31, Gender was ranked twelfth with **RII** of 3.25, Age was

ranked thirteenth with **RII** of 3.13, Education was ranked fourteenth with

RII of 3.00.

4.4.2 Civil servants Importance Index for the ministry of physical planning and development unit

Table 17. **Civil servants Importance Index for the ministry of physical planning and development unit**

S/N	Factors	VI	I	SWI	NI	NAI	TWV	(RII)	RANK
1	Salary	3	5	1	-	-	38	4.22	2
2	Marital status	1	6	2	-	-	35	3.89	6
3	Parental home ownership	2	3	4	-	-	34	3.78	8
4	Tribe	-	4	-	-	-	31	3.44	11
5	Gender	1	3	5	-	-	32	3.56	10
6	Education	1	2	4	-	2	27	3.00	13
7	Age	1	2	4	-	2	27	3.00	14
8	Land acquisition	1	3	4	-	1	30	3.33	12
9	Land security	1	5	3	-	-	34	3.78	8
10	Family size	2	4	3	-	-	35	3.89	6
11	Loan facilities	3	5	1	-	-	38	4.22	2
12	Lending rate	2	5	2	-	-	36	4.00	5
13	Costs of building materials	5	2	1	-	1	37	4.11	4
14	Personal priority	5	2	2	-	-	39	4.33	1
15	Others	-	-	-	-	-	-	-	-
	Mean of $\sum$RII = 52.5/14 = 3.75								

Key: *VI- Very influential, I-Influential, SWI- Somewhat influential, NI- Not Influential, NAI- Not at all influential, TWV-Total Weighted Value, RII-* **Relative Importance Index, ministry of physical planning and development unit.**
Source: Author's field work, 2016.

As indicated in the table above, Personal priority was ranked first with **RII** of 4.33

amongst the factors, this shows that the priority of the civil servants in this ministry is factor

that determine the whether the civil servants prioritizes home or some other things known to them. Salary and loan facilities were ranked second with **RII** of 4.22, Costs of building materials was ranked fourth with **RII** of 4.11, Lending rate was ranked fifth with **RII** of 4.00, Family size and Marital status was ranked sixth with **RII** of 3.89, Land security Parental home ownership was ranked eighth with **RII** of 3.78, Gender was ranked tenth with **RII** of 3.56, Tribe was ranked eleventh with **RII** of 3.44, Land acquisition was ranked twelfth with **RII** of 3.33, Education was ranked thirteenth with **RII** of 3.31, Age was ranked fourteenth with **RII** of 3.00.

4.4.3 Civil servants Importance Index for the ministry of Land, housing and survey

Table 18. **Civil servants Importance Index for the ministry of Land, housing and survey**

S/N	Factors	VI	I	SWI	NI	NAI	TWV	(RII)	RANK
1	Salary	13	10	-	1	1	108	4.32	2
2	Marital status	6	15	2	2	-	100	4.00	5
3	Parental home ownership	4	10	8	1	1	87	3.63	10
4	Tribe	3	6	11	2	2	111	4.44	1
5	Gender	4	6	12	1	2	84	3.36	12
6	Education	4	4	11	2	3	76	3.17	14
7	Age	3	5	13	2	2	80	3.20	13
8	Land acquisition	4	11	5	1	2	83	3.61	9
9	Land security	5	13	3	2	1	91	3.79	6
10	Family size	5	13	3	1	2	90	3.75	7
11	Loan facilities	8	9	2	3	3	91	3.64	8
12	Lending rate	4	11	4	1	4	82	3.42	11
13	Costs of building materials	11	9	2	2	1	102	4.08	3
14	Personal priority	10	10	3	1	1	102	4.08	3
15	Others	-	-	-	-	-	-	-	
	Mean of $\sum$RII = 52.5/14 = 3.75								

Key: *VI- Very influential, I-Influential, SWI- Somewhat influential, NI- Not Influential, NAI- Not at all influential, TWV-Total Weighted Value, RII- Relative Importance Index,* **ministry of Land, housing and survey.**
Source: Author's field work, 2016.

As indicated in the table above, Tribe was ranked first with **RII** of 4.44 amongst the factors, this indicate that some are of the believe that some tribes hold owning a home a necessity while some tribes does not, and those that sees it as a necessity will put all possible resources together to achieve that. Salary was ranked second with **RII** of 4.32, Costs of building materials and Personal priority were ranked third with **RII** of 4.08, Marital status was ranked fifth with **RII** of 4.00, Land security was ranked sixth with **RII** of 3.79, Family size was ranked seventh with **RII** of 3.75, Loan facilities was ranked eighth with **RII** of 3.64, Land acquisition was ranked ninth with **RII** of 3.61, Parental home ownership was ranked tenth with **RII** of 3.63, Lending rate was ranked eleventh with **RII** of 3.42, Gender was ranked twelfth with **RII** of 3.36, Age was ranked thirteenth with **RII** of 3.20, Education was ranked fourteenth with **RII** of 3.17.

4.4.4 Civil servants Importance Index for the ministry of Local government and chieftaincy matter

Table 19. Civil servants Importance Index for the ministry of Local government and chieftaincy matter

S/N	Factors	VI	I	SWI	NI	NAI	TWV	(RII)	RANK
1	Salary	9	4	-	-	-	61	4.69	1
2	Marital status	3	7	2	-	1	50	3.85	4
3	Parental home ownership	1	4	5	1	2	40	3.08	12
4	Tribe	1	-	9	1	2	36	2.78	14
5	Gender	1	2	7	1	2	38	2.92	13
6	Education	1	4	7	-	1	44	3.38	10
7	Age	1	5	5	1	1	43	3.31	11
8	Land acquisition	2	9	1	-	1	50	3.85	4
9	Land security	3	7	1	-	2	48	3.69	6
10	Family size	4	5	-	1	2	44	3.67	8
11	Loan facilities	3	7	1	-	2	48	3.69	6
12	Lending rate	2	6	3	-	1	45	3.46	9
13	Costs of building materials	7	5	-	1	-	57	4.38	2
14	Personal priority	7	3	1	-	2	52	4.00	3
15	Others	-	-	-	-	-	-	-	
	Mean of $\sum$RII = 50.82/14 = 3.63								

Key: *VI- Very influential, I-Influential, SWI- Somewhat influential, NI- Not Influential, NAI- Not at all influential, TWV-Total Weighted Value, RII-* Relative Importance Index, ministry of Local government and chieftaincy matter.
Source: Author's field work, 2016.

As indicated in the table above, Salary was ranked first with **RII** of 4.69 amongst the factors, this reveals that salary is a major determinant for civil servants to own a home and the higher their salary, the higher their savings which boost their chances of owning a home. Costs of building materials was ranked second with **RII** of 4.38, Personal priority was ranked third with **RII** of 4.00, Marital status and Land acquisition were ranked fourth with **RII** of 3.85, Land security and loan facilities were ranked sixth with **RII** of 3.69, Family size was ranked eighth with **RII** of 3.67, Lending rate was ranked ninth with **RII** of 3.46, Education

was ranked tenth with **RII** of 3.38, Age was ranked eleventh with **RII** of 3.31, Parental home

ownership was ranked twelfth with **RII** of 3.08, Gender was ranked thirteenth with **RII** of

2.92, Tribe was ranked fourteenth with **RII** of 2.78.

4.4.5 Civil servants Importance Index for the ministry of youths and sport

Table 20. **Civil servants Importance Index for the ministry of youths and sport**

S/N	Factors	VI	I	SWI	NI	NAI	TWV	(RII)	RANK
1	Salary	22	7	1	-	1	142	4.58	2
2	Marital status	12	11	7	-	-	125	4.17	3
3	Parental home ownership	4	8	16	-	3	103	3.32	13
4	Tribe	2	8	17	-	4	97	3.13	14
5	Gender	6	10	11	-	4	107	3.45	12
6	Education	6	10	12	-	12	108	3.60	11
7	Age	6	11	11	-	2	109	3.63	10
8	Land acquisition	5	18	6	-	1	119	3.84	5
9	Land security	3	16	12	-	-	116	3.87	4
10	Family size	3	16	12	-	-	155	3.70	9
11	Loan facilities	5	16	10	-	-	119	3.84	5
12	Lending rate	5	15	10	-	1	116	3.74	7
13	Costs of building materials	18	12	-	-	-	138	4.60	1
14	Personal priority	9	12	2	3	3	108	3.72	8
15	Others	-	-	-	-	-	-	-	

Mean of $\sum$RII = 53.06/14 = **3.79**

Key: *VI- Very influential, I-Influential, SWI- Somewhat influential, NI- Not Influential, NAI- Not at all influential, TWV-Total Weighted Value, RII- Relative Importance Index, ministry of youths and sport.*
Source: Author's field work, 2016.

As indicated in the table above, Costs of building materials was ranked first with **RII**

of 4.60 amongst the factors, this reveal that the more affordable the cost of building materials

are, the more the civil servants will be encouraged to embark on construction of home.

Salary was ranked second with **RII** of 4.58, Marital status was ranked third with **RII** of 4.17,

Land security was ranked fourth with **RII** of 3.87, Land acquisition and loan facilities were ranked fifth with **RII** of 3.84, Lending rate was ranked seventh with **RII** of 3.74, Personal priority was ranked eighth with **RII** of 3.72, Family size was ranked ninth with **RII** of 3.70, Age was ranked tenth with **RII** of 3.70, Education was ranked eleventh with **RII** of 3.60, Gender was ranked twelfth with **RII** of 3.45, Parental home ownership was ranked thirteenth with **RII** of 3.32 Tribe was ranked fourteenth with **RII** of 3.13.

4.4.6 Civil servants Importance Index for the five (5) ministries

Table 21. **Civil servants Importance Index for the five (5) ministries**

S/N	Factors	VI	I	SWI	NI	NAI	TWV	(RII)	RANK
1	Salary	54	36	2	1	2	424	4.46	4
2	Marital status	22	52	17	2	1	374	3.98	5
3	Parental home ownership	14	28	42	2	7	319	3.43	11
4	Tribe	7	25	51	3	8	335	3.53	10
5	Gender	13	25	47	2	8	318	3.35	12
6	Education	13	23	45	4	8	308	3.31	14
7	Age	12	27	43	3	8	311	3.34	13
8	Land acquisition	15	49	21	1	6	430	4.57	2
9	Land security	16	53	17	2	5	354	3.78	7
10	Family size	16	43	27	2	5	342	3.68	8
11	Loan facilities	23	46	17	3	6	3.62	3.81	6
12	Lending rate	16	46	23	1	8	343	3.65	9
13	Costs of building materials	53	29	5	3	3	438	4.66	1
14	Personal priority	36	33	9	4	8	410	4.51	3
15	Others	-	-	-	-	-	-	-	
	Mean of $\sum$**RII = 54.04/14 = 3.86**								

Key: *VI- Very influential, I-Influential, SWI- Somewhat influential, NI- Not Influential, NAI- Not at all influential, TWV-Total Weighted Value, RII- Relative Importance Index, the five (5) ministries.*
Source: Author's field work, 2016.

As indicated in the table above, Costs of building materials was ranked first with **RII** of 4.66 amongst the factors, this reveal that the more affordable the cost of building materials are, the more the civil servants will be encouraged to embark on construction of home. Land acquisition was ranked second with **RII** of 4.57, Personal priority was ranked third with **RII** of 4.51, Salary was ranked fourth with **RII** of 4.46, Marital status was ranked fifth with **RII** of 3.98, Loan facilities was ranked sixth with **RII** of 3.81, Land security was ranked seventh **RII** of 3.78, Lending rate was ranked ninth with **RII** of 3.65, Tribe was ranked tenth with **RII** of 3.53, Parental home ownership was ranked eleventh with **RII** of 3.43, Gender was ranked twelfth with **RII** of 3.35, Age was ranked thirteenth with **RII** of 3.34, Education was ranked fourteenth with **RII** of 3.31.

CHAPTER FIVE

SUMMARY OF FINDINGS, RECOMMENDATIONS AND CONCLUSION

5.1 Summary of Findings

The aim of this research was to examine the factors influencing homeownership amongst civil servants in Ibadan metropolis, Oyo state. The objectives of the research are to evaluate the socio-economic characteristics of homeowners, examine housing preferences of homeowners, examine and identify the factors affecting aspiring homeowners in the study area.

The study revealed that 17.9% of the respondents were from the Ministry of Establishment and Training, 13.7% of the respondents were from the Ministry of Local Government and Chieftaincy Matters, 26.3% were from the Ministry of Land, Housing and Survey, 36.2% were from the Ministry of Youth and Sport while 9.5% of the respondents were from Ministry of Physical Planning and Development Unit.

Respondents with 1-5 years of service were 10.5%, 6-10 years were 36.2%, 11-15 years were 34.7%, and 16-20 years were 3.2%, while respondents with 21 and above years of experience are 18.9% of the total respondents surveyed.

The survey revealed that the percentage of 'junior staffs' was 54.7% while that of the 'senior staff' was 45.3%, the survey further revealed that the percentage of respondents that were ''below 20 years'' was 1.1%, '21-30 years' was 29.5%, '31-40 years' was 36.8%, '41-50 years' was 26.3%, '51 years and above' was 6.3%. It was established that 25.3% of the respondents were single while 74.7% were married. The survey also revealed that respondents with the academic qualification of 'National Diploma' were 47.4%, 'Higher

National Diploma' were 29.5%, 'Bachelor of Science' were 15.8%, 'Master of Science' were 4.2%, and 'others' were 3.2%. it was established that the percentage of respondents within the salary range of '₦31,000-₦50,000' was 39.8%, '₦51,000-₦70,000' was 17.9%, '₦71,000-₦90,000' was 28.4%, '₦91,000 and above' was 14.7% . The survey revealed that the percentage of respondents within the family size range of '1 -2' were 26.3%, '3 -4'were 53.7%, and '5 -6'were 20.0% of the total respondents.

The second objective was to examine housing preferences of homeowners in the study areas revealed that the housing preferences of respondents are as follows, Duplex was ranked first with **RPI** of 4.97 amongst the preferences. Condominium was ranked second with **RPI** of 4.62, Flat was ranked third with **RPI** of 4.42, Detached house was ranked fourth with **RPI** of 4.38, Bungalow was ranked fifth with **RPI** of 4.19, Semi-detached was ranked sixth with **RPI** of 3.66, Terrace house was ranked seventh **RPI** of 3.24, Tenement house was ranked eighth with **RPI** of 3.19, Row house was ranked ninth with **RPI** of 2.35.

The third objective is identifying and examining the factors affecting aspiring homeowners, and the survey revealed that the factors influencing the respondents for Costs of building materials was ranked first with **RII** of 4.66 amongst the factors. Land acquisition was ranked second with **RII** of 4.57, Personal priority was ranked third with **RII** of 4.51, Salary was ranked fourth with **RII** of 4.46, Marital status was ranked fifth with **RII** of 3.98, Loan facilities was ranked sixth with **RII** of 3.81, Land security was ranked seventh **RII** of 3.78, Lending rate was ranked ninth with **RII** of 3.65, Tribe was ranked tenth with **RII** of 3.53, Parental home ownership was ranked eleventh with **RII** of 3.43, Gender was ranked twelfth with **RII** of 3.35, Age was ranked thirteenth with **RII** of 3.34, Education was ranked fourteenth with **RII** of 3.31.

5.2 Recommendations

This work recommends that in other to improve and increase homeowners amongst civil servants, government should implement a policy that will make cost of building materials affordable (rebate for importers of building materials), ensure that civil servants salaries are upwardly reviewed as at when and paid promptly, should ensure the mortgage institutions in the country are citizens-friendly, efficient and effective, government should also implement a policy that will make land affordable and secured, and provision of housing loans at a relatively low lending rate should be implemented. These will really help increase number of homeowners the study area.

5.3 Conclusion

This study concluded that the housing preferences of prospective and existing homeowners of the civil servants in the Ibadan metropolis are rated in the hierarchical sequence of Duplex, Condominium, Flat house, detached house, Bungalow, Semi-detached house, Terrace house, Tenement house and Row houses.

While factors influencing homeownership amongst civil in the study are rated in terms of hierarchical sequence in the order of Costs of building materials, Land acquisition, Personal priority, Salary, Marital status, Loan facilities, Land security, Family size, lending rate, Tribe, Parental home ownership, Gender, Age, Education and Others.

REFERENCES

Adekemi, E. O. (2013). Challenges of Housing Delivery in Metropolitan Lagos, *Research on humanities and social science*, 3.

Agbakoba.O. (2015). Housing shortage, *interview*. Lagos, Nigeria, Punchng.com.

Agboola T. (2000). Housing, poverty and environment – the Nigerian situation. *A seminar paper presented at a workshop on effective approach to housing delivery in Nigeria*. Organized by the Nigerian institute of building, Ibadan, Nigeria.

Agbola, S.B. (1988). The Housing of Nigerians: A review of policy development and implementation, Research Reports, Ibadan, Nigeria, 14, *Development Policy Centre*.

Akeju, A. A. (2007) *Challenges to Providing Affordable Housing in Nigeria*. Paper Presented at 2nd Emerging Urban Africa International Conference on Housing Finance in Nigeria. Held at SheuYa-adua Centre, Abuja, Nigeria. October 17th – 19th 2007.

Amdii, I. E. S. (1993) *Analysis of Government Policies in Nigeria. Zaria*, Nigeria, Amadu Bello University 1 (1) 53-63.

Aribigbola, A. (2006). Rational Choice Model and Housing Decisions in Akure, Ondo State Nigeria, *Confluence Journal of Environmental Studies*, 1 (1), 53-63.

Andrew Haughwout, R. P. (2009). The homeownership gap, *Federal Reserve Bank of New York*, 16, 5.

Bana, P.M. (1991). Housing the Urban Poor in Nigeria, *Nigerian Institute of Architects*, 6(1), 22-25.

Bazylann, M. (2009). *Factor influencing tenure choice in European Countries,* department of Applied Econometrics, Warsaw School of Economics, Berlin, 1-9.

Cabrera, J. A. (2012). The determinants of Homeownership in presence of shocks experienced by Mexican Households, *Agricultural Economics*, Mexico, 20-30.

Carlos Garriga, W. T. (2006). Recent Trends in Homeownership, *Federal Reserve Bank of St. Louis Reviw,* September/October, 88(5), 379-411.

Chukwujekwu, I.E. (2006) Facilitating Low Cost Housing Scheme: Which Way Forward? *The Journal of the Association of Housing Corporations of Nigeria*, 1(10).

Di Salvo P, Ermisch J, (1997). Analysis of dynamics of housing tenure choice in Britain, *Journal of Urban Economics*, 42, 1-17.

Drew, R. B. (2014). Believing in Homeownership: Behavioral drivers of Housing Tenure decisions. *Joint Center for Housing Studies,* Harvard University, London, 5-12.

Edgar, B. (2007). Homeownership and Marginalisation, *Bulgaria: European Journal of Homelessness*, 1, 141-148.

Emerole, C.G. (2002). Restructuring Housing Development and Financing in Nigeria: *The role of Partnership and Collaboration Strategies*, Housing Today 1(5), 26-29.

Festus, I. A. (2015). Housing policy in Nigeria: An overview. *American International Journal of Contemporary Research*, 5.

Fetter, D. K. (2013). How Do Mortgage Subsidies Affect Home Ownership Mid-Century GI Bills, *American Economic Journal: Economic Policy,* 5(2), 111–147.

Fishback, P. V. (2009). *The Influence of the Home Owners' Loan Corporation on Housing Markets During the 1930s* . Economic History Association, 4-44.

Gandelman, N. (2005). Homeownership and Gender, Latin American Research Network Uruguay, 2-16

Gary Painter, L. Y. (2002). Heterogeneity in Asian American Homeownership: The impact of Household Endowments and immigrant status, *USC Lusk Center Working* , Los Angeles, 1010-2001.

Gyourko, J. & Linneman, P. (1996). Analysis of the Changing Influences on Traditional Households' Ownership Patterns, *Journal of Urban Economics* 39(3), 318-341.

Ikejiofor, U. (2005). *Land issues in the new National housing policy for Nigeria: Lessons from research experience*, Liverpool University Press. Retrieved http://www.deepdyve.com/liverpool-university-press

Haurin, Donald R. & K. B. Lee. (1989). A Structural Model of the Demand for Owner-Occupied Housing, *Journal of Urban Economics*, 26, 348-360.

Haurin, Donald R., Toby Parcel & R. Jean Haurin. (2002). Does Home Ownership Affect Child Outcomes, Real Estate Economics, 30, 635-666.

Hood. (2002). The determinants of Homeownership: An Application of the Human Capital Investment Theory to the Home Ownership Decision, *The Park Economist,* 7.

Jamison, A. B. (2011). Shift confidence in Homeownership: The Great Recession, *Federal Reserve Bank of Boston*, 1-40.

Joseph. (1996). Study on housing demand, *Research and Library Services Division*, 5-20.

Nnamdi, P. C. (2013). Income Status and Homeownership: Micro-econometric Evidence. Enugu: *West African Journal of Industrial and Academic Research* 8.

Obunadike, G.O. (2003). *Land Administrative in Anambra State, Paper presented at the working luncheon organized by NIESV*, Anambra State Branch at Tracy Hotels, Akwa.

Olotuah, A.O & Bobadoye, S.A. (2009). Sustainable housing provision for the urban poor: A review of public sector intervention in Nigeria, *The built and human environment review*, 3, 42-48.

Oluwatobi, C. A. (2011). Issues and challenges Millitating against the sustainability of affordable Housing Privison in Nigeria, *Business Management Dynamics*, 1(4), Oct 2011, 01-08.

Omirin, M.M. (2002). *Issues in land accessibility in Nigeria, Proceedings of a national workshop on land management and property tax reform in Nigeria*, Department of Estate Management, University of Lagos, Nigeria.

Rohe, W. M. & V. Basolo. 1997. Environment and Behavior, *Long-Term Effects of Homeownership on the Self-Perceptions and Social Interaction of Low-Income Persons*, 29(6), 793-819.

Rohe, W. M. & M. Stegman. 1994. Urban Affairs Quarterly, *the Impact of Home Ownership on the Social and Political Involvement of Low-Income People*. 30, 152-172.

Rowlingson, L. A. (2010). *Homeownership and the distribution of personal wealth.* Housing
Market Taskforce, 4, 4-30.

Samson, D. (2004). The sustainability of Homeownership: Factors affecting the duration of
Homeownership and rental spells, *U.S. Department of Housing and Urban
Development Office of Policy Development and Research,* 7, 20-62.

Sullivan, L. M. (2005). Trends in homeownership: Race, Demographics and Income, *nsw
parliamentary research service,* Chicago,

Wachter, S. M., & Megbolugbe, I. F. (1992). Impacts of housing and mortgage market
discrimination racial and ethnic disparities in homeownership. *Housing Policy
Debate*, 3(2), 332-370.

Xhignesse, G. (2012). What are the determinants of Homeownerhip, *Research Center in
Urban Sciences, University of Liège, Belgium,* 4-15.

DEPARTMENT OF ESTATE MANAGEMENT
FACULTY OF ENVIRONMENTAL DESIGN AND MANAGEMENT
OBAFEMI AWOLOWO UNIVERSITY, ILE IFE, OSUN STATE

QUESTIONNAIRE

TOPIC: FACTORS INFLUENCING HOME OWNERSHIP AMONGST CIVIL SERVANTS IN IBADAN METROPOLIS.

Dear Sir/Madam,

This questionnaire is designed to collect information on the **Factors Influencing Home ownership amongst Civil servants in Ibadan Metropolis, Oyo State.** It is a final year undergraduate dissertation. All information given is for academic purpose and as such will be treated with utmost confidentiality.

Thanks for your anticipated cooperation.

Yours Faithfully
OJEKUNLE, Olabisi Sunday

****Please fill and tick (✓) as appropriate in the spaces provided for each question****

SECTION A: PROFILE OF RESPONDENT

1. Name of Ministry..

2. Number of years in service... (a) 1-5 years [ ] (b) 6-10 years [ ] (c) 11-15 years [ ]
   (d) 16-20 years [ ] (e) 21 and above [ ]

3. Status of Respondent: (a) ad hoc staffs [ ] (b) Junior staffs (c) Senior staffs
   (d) Permanent secretary (e) Others, please specify ....

4. Age of respondent (a) below 20 years (b) 21-30 years [ ] (c) 31-40 years [ ]
   (d) 41-50 years [ ] (e) 51 years and above [ ]

5. Gender of respondent (a) Male [ ] (b) Female [ ]

6. Marital status of respondent (a) Single [ ] (b) Married [ ]

7. Academic qualification (a) N.D [ ] (b) H.N.D [ ] (c) B.Sc. [ ] (d) M.Sc. [ ] (e) Ph.D [ ]
   others, please specify..

8. Salary range (a)N10,000-N30,000 [ ] (b) N31,000-N50,000 [ ] (c) N51,000-N70,000 [ ]
    (d) N71,000-N90,000 [ ] (e) N91,000 and above [ ]
9. Family size (a)1 -2 [ ] (b)3 -4 [ ] (c)5 -6 [ ] (d)7 -8 [ ] (e)9 - above [ ]

SECTION B: EXAMINING FACTORS INFLUENCING HOMEOWNERSHIP

Please mark the degree of acceptance in the table below

S/No.	Factors	Degree acceptance				
		(a) Highly preferred	(b) preferred	(c) Somewhat preferred	(d) Not preferred	(e) Not at all preferred
1.	Salary					
2.	Marital status					
3.	Parental home ownership					
4.	Tribe					
5.	Gender					
6.	Education					
7.	Age					
8.	Land acquisition					
9.	Land security					
10.	Family size					
11.	Loan facilities					
12.	Lending rate					
13.	Costs of building materials					
14.	Personal priority					
15.	Others, specify ………………					

SECTION C: EXAMINING HOUSING PREFERENCES OF HOMEOWNERSHIP

Please mark the degree of acceptance in the table below

S/No.	Preferences	Degree acceptance				
		(a) Very influential	(b)Influential	(c) Somewhat influential	(d) Not influential	(e) Not at all influential
1.	Bungalow					
2.	Detached house					
3.	Semi-detached					
4.	Terrace house					
5.	Tenement house					
6.	Duplex					
7.	Condominium					
8.	Flat					
9.	Row house					
10.	Others, specify ………...........………..